time to
SLEEP

Written and Illustrated by

Steve Jenkins and Robin Page

Houghton Mifflin Books for Children • Houghton Mifflin Harcourt • Boston New York 2011

Like you, animals need to sleep. But they get their rest in lots of different ways. There are animals that sleep during the day, and others that snooze after the sun goes down. A few just take short naps, but some may be awake for only a few hours a day. There are animals that lie down to sleep, and creatures that doze while standing, hanging upside down, floating in the water — even flying.

Once I get down here, it's hard to get up.

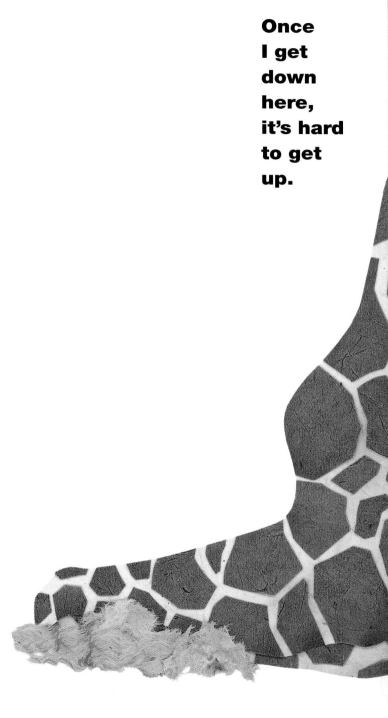

The **giraffe** sleeps less than two hours each day. It can sleep standing up or lying down, curled into a ball.

It's Tuesday already?

Snug in its underground
burrow, the **hairy armadillo**
snoozes for more than
twenty hours a day.

To stay warm, the red fox
sleeps with its long, bushy tail
wrapped around its nose.

Heads . . .

. . . or tails?

Scoot over,
       please.

Bee-eaters line up to sleep. Those at either end, however, stay awake and watch for danger. The birds take turns standing guard, changing places so that every bird gets a chance to rest.

Early warning system

The **basilisk** falls asleep balanced on a thin branch that hangs over the water. If a snake approaches, the branch shakes and the lizard wakes up, drops into the water, and swims to safety.

My foot's asleep!

To stay safe from predators, the **flamingo** sleeps standing in shallow water. As it dozes, the bird conserves body heat by standing on one leg and tucking the other leg into its feathers. From time to time, it switches legs.

Each night the **parrotfish** produces a mucus cocoon that surrounds its body. This slimy coating conceals the parrotfish's scent from predators, keeping it safe as it sleeps.

A slimy sleeping bag

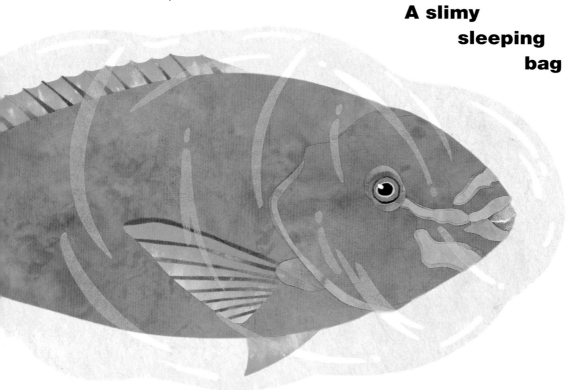

Before dozing off, the **warthog** wriggles backwards into a cave or crevice in the rock. Its sharp tusks face outward as it sleeps.

**Get
the
point?**

The **green sea turtle** sinks to the sea floor to sleep. All turtles breathe air, but the green sea turtle can hold its breath for a long time. Still, after an hour or two, it must wake up and swim to the surface to breathe.

Time to get a little fresh air

Snoozing
on autopilot

The **white stork** sleeps in flight.
Scientists believe it does this by
taking a series of naps that last
just a few seconds each.

When autumn arrives, the **European hedgehog** crawls into its burrow and wraps itself into a spiky ball. There it falls into an especially deep sleep, called hibernation, that will last for months.

Don't touch!

Brrr.

The **wood frog** passes the winter resting
on the forest floor. There, in an unusual
form of hibernation, it freezes solid,
turning into what looks like a lumpy green
ice cube covered with frost. It will thaw
out in the spring.

Sleeping, or just holding on?

Long-horned bees hang motionless through the night, holding tight to a twig or leaf. It's not known if bees actually sleep — perhaps they are just resting.

When you come to a fork in the tree . . .

At bedtime, the **koala** sometimes wedges itself between the branches of a tree so it won't tumble out in its sleep.

Hanging out

The **walrus** isn't choosy about where it beds down. It naps on the sea floor, sleeps as it drifts along on the ocean's surface, or snoozes on the beach. Sometimes it just hangs out, supported by an ice floe and its long tusks.

Split personality

Like all mammals, the **bottlenose dolphin** breathes air. As it sleeps, one half of its brain stays awake to tell the dolphin when it's time to surface and take a breath. The two halves of its brain take turns sleeping.

Where will *you* fall asleep tonight?

Sleep tight . . .

Gorillas like to snuggle. Every night, they make a big nest of leaves and grass, then gather in a sleepy pile.

To learn more about the animals in this book, turn the page.

At a height of 19 feet (6 meters), the **giraffe** is the world's tallest animal. Giraffes graze in small groups — called herds, corps, or towers — on the open grasslands of Africa. The giraffe often feeds on foliage that is too high for other animals to reach. It is especially fond of acacia trees, and uses its long tongue to carefully pluck leaves growing among the tree's sharp thorns.

The **hairy armadillo** is about 12 inches (30 centimeters) long. This armored mammal shuffles about the grasslands and open woodlands of South America. It eats insects, fruit, nuts, and dead animals. It digs a burrow with its powerful claws, and spends much of its time sleeping underground. Like all armadillos, it can protect itself against predators by curling up into a ball.

The **red fox** is a relative of the domestic dog. A large red fox can weigh more than 20 pounds (9 kilograms), but most are smaller. There are dozens of different kinds of foxes, found almost everywhere on earth. Foxes are omnivores. They prefer to hunt live prey, including rodents, birds, and reptiles, but they will also eat fruit, vegetables, and garbage.

The **European bee-eater** nests in the warm parts of Europe but migrates thousands of miles each year to tropical habitats in Africa. Bee-eaters, which are about 11 inches (28 centimeters) long, are social birds. They flock in meadows and other open landscapes where they feed on insects, including bees and wasps. They always take their prey on the wing — if an insect isn't flying, the bee-eater ignores it. Before it eats a bee or wasp, the bird holds the insect in its beak and rubs or pounds it on a tree branch until the insect's stinger comes off. The bee-eater can catch and eat as many as 250 bees a day.

The **basilisk** lives in the rainforests of Central America. It spends much of its time in trees, but never strays far from water. This lizard is about 12 inches (30 centimeters) long, and eats insects, leaves, fruit, and small animals. It is famous for being able to sprint across the surface of the water. Flaps of skin on its back feet trap pockets of air beneath its toes, holding the animal up as it runs, an ability that gives the basilisk its nickname of "the Jesus Christ lizard."

The **flamingo** is famous for its bright pink color, but a captive flamingo fed ordinary bird food turns a dull gray. The bird's intense color comes from its diet of shrimp and other small marine animals. Flamingo colonies, which can include thousands of birds, flock near fresh or salt water in tropical environments throughout the world. The flamingo spends most of its waking hours wading in the shallows, straining small animals from the water with its beak. Flamingos are large birds, standing as tall as four feet (122 centimeters).

The teeth of the **parrotfish** have fused to form a sort of beak. The fish, which lives on coral reefs throughout the world, uses its beak to bite off chunks of coral. The fish eats the soft polyps living inside and grinds the hard coral shell to powder. Much of the fine sand found on tropical beaches and sea floors is coral that has been pulverized and excreted by parrotfish. These colorful fish range in length from one to four feet (30–122 centimeters).

The **warthog,** a relative of the domestic pig, lives in the forests and grasslands of central and southern Africa. It feeds on leaves, fruit, bark, insects, and small animals. The warthog's large head and long, curving tusks make it look awkward, but it can move with surprising speed and agility. Warthogs can weigh as much as 300 pounds (136 kilograms). They are good diggers, but they will often use burrows dug by aardvarks rather than excavating their own.

Weighing as much as 700 pounds (318 kilograms) and measuring up to five feet (1½ meters) in length, the **green sea turtle** is one of the world's largest turtles. It lives in warm ocean waters throughout the world and leaves the sea only to lay its eggs on land. Adult green sea turtles are herbivores — they feed on seaweed and algae. Young turtles, however, are predators. They hunt jellyfish and other soft marine creatures. The turtle's name comes not from the color of its shell, which is often more brown than green, but from the green fat found beneath its skin.

The **white stork** can stand 50 inches (127 centimeters) tall. It is a wading bird that lives near lakes, marshes, and rivers. Its diet includes frogs, snakes, fish, insects, and small reptiles and mammals. These large birds nest in Europe, the Middle East, and parts of Asia, but they are long-distance fliers and migrate thousands of miles to spend the winter in South Africa or India. Many people believe that having a white stork nest on one's home or land is a sign of good fortune, so the birds are rarely hunted.

The **European hedgehog** lives in woods, farmlands, and meadows throughout Europe. Its body, which is about 10 inches (25 centimeters) long, is covered with thousands of sharp spines. The hedgehog can't move very fast. Instead, it curls itself into a ball to protect itself from predators. During the warm months, hedgehogs are active at night. They use their keen sense of smell to hunt for insects, worms, spiders, frogs, young birds, and small mammals. In the winter, they fall into a deep sleep and hibernate in an underground burrow.

The **wood frog** is found throughout much of the northern United States and Canada. It is a small frog, only about two inches (5 centimeters) long. This amphibian eats insects and other invertebrates it finds among the litter on the forest floor. Wood frogs are best known for their ability to withstand being frozen solid. Normally when animals freeze, ice crystals form in their tissues and cause fatal damage. The wood frog, however, has a special kind of "antifreeze" in its body that prevents the formation of ice crystals.

Long-horned bees get their name from the male bee's long antennae. These insects are found in many parts of Europe and North America. Like most bees, they feed on flower nectar and are important pollinators of many plants. They are about the same size as a honeybee — half an inch (12½ millimeters) long. A male long-horned bee sometimes grasps a flower or blade of grass and hangs on, motionless, through the night. Is it asleep? An insect's brain is so different from a human's that we don't really know.

The **koala** lives in the forests of eastern Australia. These tree-dwelling mammals are marsupials, and the females carry and nurse their young — which are born blind and helpless — in a pouch. A koala looks like a small bear, and some people even call them "koala bears," but they are more closely related to opossums and kangaroos. Koalas average about 20 pounds (9 kilograms) in weight. Their diet consists almost entirely of the leaves of the eucalyptus tree. These leaves are not very nutritious, so the koala spends most of its waking time eating. It saves energy by sleeping as much as eighteen hours a day.

The **walrus** is a large marine mammal that lives in the cold ocean waters of the northern Atlantic and Pacific oceans. A large male walrus can weigh more than 4,000 pounds (1,814 kilograms).

Females are smaller, but both males and females have a pair of tusks that can reach three feet (91 centimeters) in length. They use these tusks, which are specially adapted teeth, to fight other walruses and to drag themselves out of the water. A walrus can hold its breath for up to thirty minutes, and it spends most of its life at sea. Using its sensitive lips and whiskers, it snuffles along the bottom of the ocean, finding and eating crabs, shrimp, clams, and other sea floor animals. Walruses are social animals, and at certain times of the year thousands will gather on the same beach or rocky outcrop.

With the exception of the frigid waters of the Arctic and Antarctic, the **bottlenose dolphin** is found in all the world's oceans. Like its relatives the porpoises and whales, dolphins are mammals. They breathe air, and their babies are born alive and nursed with their mother's milk. Bottlenose dolphins are typically eight to twelve feet (2½ to 3½ meters) long. Dolphins eat fish and squid. They are very intelligent animals that communicate with each other by making a series of clicks, squeaks, and whistles. We don't understand what they are saying, but we know that they work together to herd schools of fish into a ball, making them easier to catch. Dolphins can also use sound to "see" prey or other objects in dark or murky water. They make rapid clicking noises and listen for the echoes. This is called *echolocation* — it's the same technique bats use to navigate in the dark.

The **gorilla** is the largest of the primates, a group that includes monkeys, chimps, and humans. Male gorillas may weigh more than 400 pounds (181 kilograms). Females are usually about half the size of males. These great apes live in the forests of central Africa and form family groups led by a large, dominant male. Gorillas may look fierce, but they are normally gentle animals that eat leaves, fruit, and insects. Humans have destroyed much of the gorilla's forest home and killed many of these peaceful animals. Of the three different kinds of gorilla—eastern lowland, western lowland, and mountain—the mountain gorilla is most endangered, with only about 600 animals remaining in the wild.

For Page — S.J. & R.P.

Houghton Mifflin Books for Children is an imprint of Houghton Mifflin Harcourt Publishing Company.

www.hmhbooks.com

The text of this book is set in Century Gothic.
The illustrations are torn- and cut-paper collage.

Library of Congress Cataloging-in-Publication Data

Jenkins, Steve, 1952–
  Time to sleep / written and illustrated by Steve Jenkins and Robin Page.
    p. cm.
  ISBN 978-0-547-25040-3
1. Sleep behavior in animals—Juvenile literature. I. Page, Robin, 1957– II. Title.
  QL755.3.J46 2011
  591.5'19—dc22
2010025128

Manufactured in Singapore
TWP 10 9 8 7 6 5 4 3 2 1
4500274339